All About
HENRY VIII

Anna Claybourne

raintree

Raintree is an imprint of Capstone Global Library Limited, a company incorporated in England and Wales
having its registered office at 7 Pilgrim Street, London, EC4V 6LB – Registered company number: 6695582

www.raintreepublishers.co.uk
myorders@raintreepublishers.co.uk

First published in 2008 as Henry's Heads: Henry VIII

This edition © Capstone Global Library Limited 2014
First published in paperback in 2015

The moral rights of the proprietor have been asserted.

Editorial: Louise Galpine, Harriet Milles, and Rachel Howells
Design: Richard Parker and Tinstar Design (www.tinstar.co.uk)
Illustrations: Steve Weston
Picture Research: Ruth Blair
Production: Victoria Fitzgerald

Originated by Capstone Global Library Ltd
Printed and bound in China by CTPS

ISBN 978 1 406 28583 3 (hardback)
18 17 16 15 14
10 9 8 7 6 5 4 3 2 1

ISBN 978 1 4062 8590 1 (paperback)
18 17 16 15 14
10 9 8 7 6 5 4 3 2 1

British Library Cataloguing in Publication Data
A full catalogue record for this book is available from the British Library.

Acknowledgements
We would like to thank the following for permission to reproduce photographs: Art Archive p. 12 (Civiche Racc
d'Arte Pavia Italy/Dagli Orti); Bridgeman pp. 5 (The Berger Collection at the Denver Art Museum, USA), 26
(British Library, London, UK), 28 (Houses of Parliament, Westminster, London, UK), 16 (Kunsthistorisches
Museum, Vienna, Austria), 8 (Lambeth Palace Library, London, UK), 20 (Louvre, Paris, France/Giraudon),
14–15 (Musee de Blois, Blois, France/Lauros/Giraudon), 10, 24, 25, 28 (National Portrait Gallery, London,
UK), 6 (Palace of Westminster, London, UK), 22 (Palazzo Barberini, Rome, Italy), 18 (Private Collection), 11,
23 (Private Collection/The Stapleton Collection), 21 (The Trustees of the Weston Park Foundation, UK);
Corbis pp. 17, 27, 28 (Bettmann), 18–19 (Patrick Ward); Mary Evans Picture Library pp. 7, 9, 13.

Cover photograph of an execution block and axe reproduced with permission of Corbis/Bettmann.

We would like to thank Bill Marriot and Lynne Bold for their invaluable help in the preparation of this book.

Every effort has been made to contact copyright holders of material reproduced in this book. Any omissions
will be rectified in subsequent printings if notice is given to the publisher.

All the Internet addresses (URLs) given in this book were valid at the time of going to press. However, due to
the dynamic nature of the Internet, some addresses may have changed, or sites may have changed or ceased
to exist since publication. While the author and publisher regret any inconvenience this may cause readers, no
responsibility for any such changes can be accepted by either the author or the publisher.

Contents

Some words are printed in bold, **like this**. You can find out what they mean on page 30. You can also look in the box at the bottom of the page where they first appear.

Who was Henry?

"OFF WITH HIS HEAD!" That's what kings and queens say in cartoons. And long ago, it really did happen. Kings and queens could have people **executed** (killed) whenever they liked.

One of the cruellest kings of England was Henry VIII. He had people executed in lots of horrible ways. Many had their head chopped off with an axe. Some were hanged, then cut into pieces. Others were burned on a bonfire!

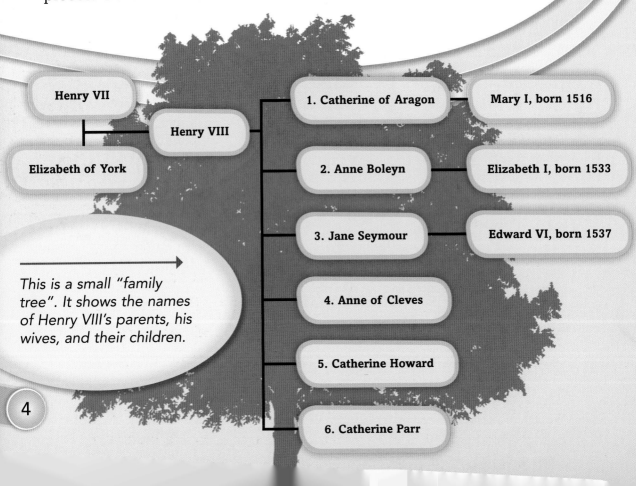

Henry VII

Elizabeth of York

Henry VIII

1. Catherine of Aragon — Mary I, born 1516

2. Anne Boleyn — Elizabeth I, born 1533

3. Jane Seymour — Edward VI, born 1537

4. Anne of Cleves

5. Catherine Howard

6. Catherine Parr

This is a small "family tree". It shows the names of Henry VIII's parents, his wives, and their children.

Henry VIII became king at the age of 17. He ruled England from 1509 to 1547.

Henry VIII ruled England nearly 500 years ago. He was the eighth English king named Henry ("VIII" means "the eighth"). He belonged to an important royal family called the Tudors. His father was Henry VII ("the seventh").

Henry didn't just chop off heads. He did many other things during his long **reign**. He married six times! He loved art and music. He was good at dancing and sport. He also changed England for ever. This book is all about Henry VIII, his six wives – and the heads he chopped off!

Henry becomes king

Henry had an older brother called Arthur. Arthur should have become king. But in 1502, Arthur fell ill and died. Now Henry would become the next king. His father, Henry VII ("seventh"), died in 1509. Henry became King Henry VIII ("eighth"). That same year, he married Catherine of Aragon – his dead brother's wife.

Wife file:
1. Catherine of Aragon

Lived: 1485–1536
Married Henry: 1509
End of marriage: marriage **annulled** in 1533
Personality: calm, sensible, loyal, clever

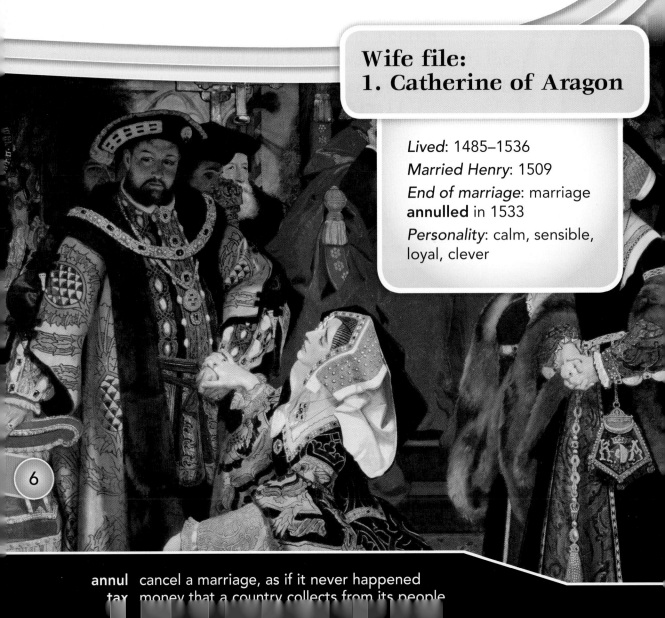

annul   cancel a marriage, as if it never happened
tax   money that a country collects from its people

Chop chop!

Who? Edmund Dudley and Richard Empson

When? 1510

Why? Dudley (left in the picture) and Empson (right) worked for Henry's father, Henry VII (seated in the middle). Everyone hated them because they made people pay lots of money in **taxes**. Henry had them killed to make people like him.

Did you know? Dudley tried to escape from prison. But he was caught and lost his head anyway.

Henry was only 17 years old when he became king. Like most teenagers, he wanted to have fun. He loved sport and games. He liked parties, fancy clothes, and riding horses. But he soon started chopping off heads, too!

The chopping block

Why did **monarchs** (kings and queens) chop off heads? It was usually because they were scared of losing their power. People often plotted against them. They wanted someone else to be king or queen. So monarchs had their enemies killed. This was a nasty warning to others!

This picture shows some enemies of Queen Isabella of France (wife of Edward II) losing their heads in about 1326.

behead   chop off someone's head
executioner   someone whose job is to execute (kill) people

Chop chop!

Who? Edward Stafford (right)

When? 1521

Why? Henry thought that Stafford was plotting against him. Henry got rid of him to stop him causing trouble.

Did you know? People said it took three swings of the axe to chop off Stafford's head.

Today, judges of the law decide punishments. But long ago, monarchs had all the power. They could do whatever they liked. If they wanted to **execute** someone, it was easy to arrange.

Beheadings happened in the open air. Anyone could go to watch. The king did not do the chopping himself. An **executioner** did it with an axe or sword. The victims could make a final speech to the crowd. Then they knelt down. Often they put their head on a special chopping block to be chopped off.

"The King's Great Matter"

Henry hoped for a son. He wanted his son to be king when he died. He and his wife Catherine had several children. Sadly, they all died, except one – a daughter called Mary.

But Henry wanted a son, not a daughter. He thought a girl could never be a good leader! Henry's hope for a son was known as "The King's Great Matter".

Princess Mary was the daughter of Henry VIII and Catherine of Aragon. She was born in 1516.

divorce   end a marriage
Pope   the leader of the Catholic Church

Henry wanted a wife who would give him a son. He decided to get rid of Catherine. But he did not chop off her head. The people of England loved Catherine. Henry did not want to upset them. Instead, he tried to **divorce** her (end their marriage).

But England belonged to the Catholic Church. The leader of the Catholic Church is the **Pope**. He did not allow divorce. Henry did not listen to the Pope. He told an English churchman, Thomas Cranmer, to **annul** (cancel) his marriage to Catherine. Henry was free!

Chop chop!

Who? Bishop John Fisher

When? 1535

Why? Fisher helped Catherine of Aragon. He tried to stop Henry's plans to divorce her. His punishment was the chop.

Did you know? John Fisher's head was stuck on a spike on London Bridge for all to see.

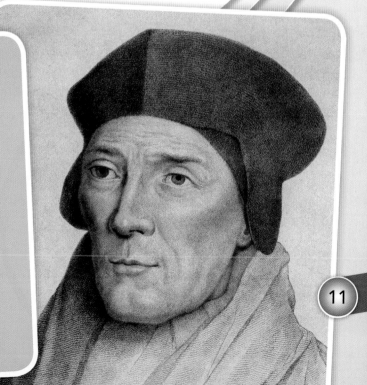

Anne Boleyn

Soon Henry had a new wife. She was a **lady-in-waiting** called Anne Boleyn. Anne was about 16 years old when she started working in Henry's palace. Everyone noticed her at once. People said that she was not pretty. But she had big dark eyes and shiny black hair. She was clever and funny. She loved dancing, parties, and fashion.

Wife file: 2. Anne Boleyn

Lived: 1507–1536
Married Henry: 1533
End of marriage: **beheaded** in 1536
Personality: clever, witty, **sharp-tongued**

lady-in-waiting maid to a queen or other rich lady
sharp-tongued making quick, harsh comments

Some people said Anne had six fingers on one hand. They said this was a sign of a witch. In those days, people believed that some women were witches. They believed they could do magic. Many of these "witches" were put to death.

Anne married Henry in 1533. But she did not give him a son. She had a daughter, called Elizabeth. This made Henry angry. To get rid of Anne, he accused her of having boyfriends. In 1536, her head was chopped off.

Chop chop!

Who? Anne Boleyn, Henry's second wife

When? 1536

Why? Henry wanted to swap Anne for a new wife. So he had several men **tortured** until they said they were Anne's boyfriend.

Did you know? Anne said that the **executioner** "... shall not have much trouble, for I have a little neck."

Anne Boleyn is taken to the Tower of London for her **execution.**

Changing the church

Henry VIII paid a big price for marrying Anne Boleyn. He had **annulled** (cancelled) his first marriage. He had broken the rules of the Catholic Church. The **Pope** was angry. He threw Henry out of the Catholic Church.

But Henry had a plan. He would set up a new Church. This new Church would be just for England. Instead of the Pope, this Church would have its own leader. And who do you think the leader would be? Henry himself, of course!

Henry got rid of the old Catholic laws. He made new laws. Now it was **treason** for anyone to say that Henry was not Head of the Church of England. Treason meant plotting against your king and country. The punishment for treason was death.

Chop chop!

Who? Sir Thomas More, Henry's **chancellor**

When? 1535

Why? Thomas More refused to agree that Henry was the new Head of the Church of England. Henry said this was treason.

Did you know? Thomas More asked the **executioner** to be careful not to chop his beard. He said his beard had not committed any crime!

chancellor senior assistant to a king or leader
treason plotting against your king or country

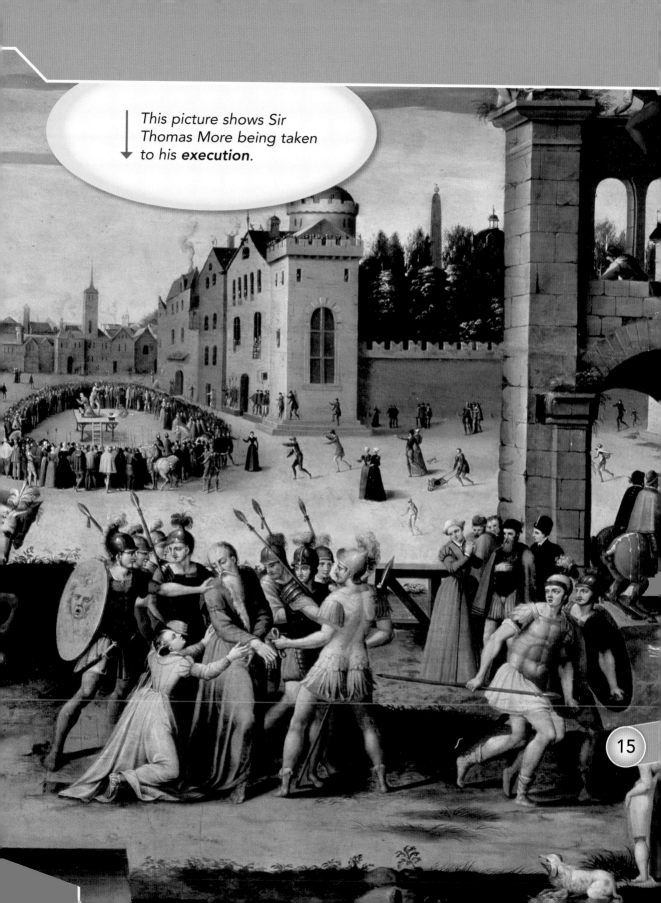

This picture shows Sir Thomas More being taken to his **execution**.

A son at last!

Just 11 days after Anne Boleyn was **beheaded**, Henry VIII had a new wife. Her name was Jane Seymour. She was another **lady-in-waiting**. Jane was much quieter than Anne. The parties at the royal palaces stopped. But Henry seemed to love Jane very much. He was happier than he had ever been.

Wife file: 3. Jane Seymour

Lived: about 1509–1537
Married Henry: 1536
End of marriage: Jane died in 1537
Personality: calm, good-natured

Best of all for Henry, Jane gave him a son. A baby boy, named Edward, was born in 1537. But Jane became very ill. She died 12 days after Edward's birth. Henry was terribly upset. He did not marry again for two years. This was a record for him! For the rest of his life, Henry always said he loved Jane best of all his wives. He was buried next to her when he died.

This is a picture of Jane and Henry's son, Edward, as a young boy. He became King Edward VI ("the sixth") when Henry VIII died.

Money and monasteries

There was more bad news for Henry VIII. He was running out of cash! He had spent too much money on palaces, parties, and fancy clothes. He had also spent too much money fighting wars – especially wars against France.

But, as always, Henry had a plan. He turned to the **monasteries**. These were places where monks lived. Monks are religious men. They spend their life following God and the Church. The monks' monasteries were full of precious books and treasure. The monasteries also owned a lot of **valuable** land.

Henry was the new Head of the Church of England. He could decide what happened to the monasteries. So he decided to steal their treasure. In the late 1530s, Henry seized the monasteries. He threw out the monks. He took their treasures and lands. This was called the "**dissolution** of the monasteries". It made Henry much richer!

dissolution   getting rid of or closing down
monastery   large house where monks live and work
valuable   worth a lot of money

This photo shows the ruins of a monastery in Whitby, Yorkshire. It was destroyed by Henry in 1539.

Chop chop!

There wasn't much chopping going on between 1537 and 1540. Henry was too busy tearing down monasteries and counting his cash.

"The Flanders mare"

Henry decided he needed another wife. His new **chancellor** was Thomas Cromwell. Cromwell had an idea. Henry could marry a princess from Cleves. Cleves was a small land in Europe (now Western Germany). Like Henry, Cleves was against the **Pope** and the Catholic Church. Henry wanted to show Cleves that England was its friend. He would marry a Cleves princess.

Henry sent an artist called Hans Holbein to Cleves. Holbein had to paint the two Cleves princesses. They were called Anne and Amelia. Henry liked Holbein's painting of Anne best (see right). He said he would marry her.

Wife file: 4. Anne of Cleves

Lived: 1515–1557
Married Henry: January 1540
End of marriage: marriage annulled July 1540
Personality: quiet, gentle, obedient

When Anne arrived in England, Henry was furious! He thought she looked nothing like Holbein's painting. He thought she was ugly. In fact, he called her "a Flanders **mare**". (Flanders was the part of Europe where Cleves was.)

But Henry had to keep his promise to Cleves. He married Anne in January 1540. But by July he had changed his mind. He **annulled** the marriage. He sent Anne to live in Hever Castle in Kent. Anne did as she was told – and kept her head.

Chop chop!

Who? Thomas Cromwell, Henry's chancellor

When? 1540

Why? Cromwell had helped Henry to marry Anne of Cleves. So Henry turned against him, even though they were close friends.

Did you know? Thomas Cromwell's **executioner** was a beginner. He did not know how to do the job properly. He kept missing. He had several tries before Cromwell's head came off!

Catherine Howard

Soon, another **lady-in-waiting** caught Henry's eye. She was Catherine Howard, Anne Boleyn's cousin. Catherine was still a teenager. Henry was almost 50 years old. He was very fat, smelly, and unhealthy. He had a wound in his leg which would not heal. This meant he could not take exercise. He also had gout. Gout is a painful disease of the feet.

· ETATIS ·

· SVÆ · XLIX ·

In later life, Henry was overweight and bloated (puffed up). This is a famous painting of him at that time.

Wife file:
5. Catherine Howard

Lived: around 1521–1542

Married Henry: 1540

End of marriage: **beheaded** in 1542

Personality: bubbly, fun-loving, full of energy

Henry gave Catherine lots of expensive gifts. He asked her to marry him. She agreed – it was hard to say no to Henry! But she did not really like him at all.

Catherine had boyfriends behind Henry's back. Henry heard about this, and Catherine was in big trouble! The boyfriends were arrested and the truth came out. Catherine faced the chop for cheating on Henry. She was only about 21 years old when she died.

Chop chop!

Who? Catherine Howard

When? 1542

Why? For having boyfriends while married to Henry.

Did you know? Catherine spent the night before her **execution** practising the best way to lay her head on the chopping block.

23

Henry's last years

Henry VIII married his last wife, Catherine Parr, in 1543. She was a widow who had been married twice before. She did not plan to marry Henry. She wanted to marry a man named Thomas Seymour. But Henry decided Catherine should marry him instead. Catherine did not have much choice!

Wife file:
6. Catherine Parr

Lived: about 1512–1548

Married Henry: 1543

End of marriage: marriage ended with Henry's death in 1547

Personality: calm, sensible, kind, clever

This picture shows Henry VIII on his death-bed (left). His son, Edward, is seated on the throne next to him.

Henry was very old, ill, and smelly. He was also going crazy. He thought people were coming to attack him in the night. Catherine Parr was a good wife to him. She looked after him kindly.

Finally, Henry VIII died, on 28 January 1547. Catherine Parr was free! She married Thomas Seymour, as she had always planned. Sadly, Catherine died a year later.

Chop chop!

Who? Henry Howard, a famous poet

When? 1547

Why? Henry VIII was dying. He was sure that Howard was plotting to grab power from his son Edward. So he wanted Howard dead.

Did you know? Henry Howard's father was also sentenced to death. Luckily for him, the king died the day before his **execution**. So he was spared the chop.

What Henry left behind

Apart from all the rolling heads, what did Henry VIII leave behind after he died?

Henry was one of England's most important **monarchs** ever. He put a great deal of money into art, music, and science. This added to a time of great art and new discoveries. This period is known as the **Renaissance**.

Henry VIII's **reign** was famous for new art, new music, and new fashions.

Renaissance   period of great exploration, art, and science in

When she was crowned queen in 1953, Queen Elizabeth II also became Head of the Church of England.

Henry also gave England its own Church – the Church of England. To this day, the king or queen of Britain is the leader of the Church of England. This is thanks to Henry VIII's laws.

Henry's children

Lastly, all three of Henry VIII's surviving children became **monarchs**, too:

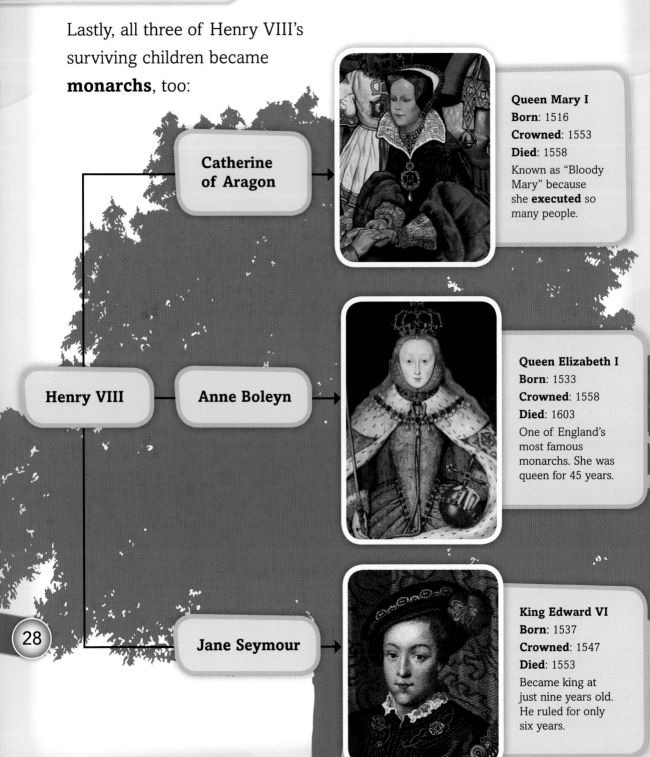

Catherine of Aragon

Queen Mary I
Born: 1516
Crowned: 1553
Died: 1558
Known as "Bloody Mary" because she **executed** so many people.

Henry VIII

Anne Boleyn

Queen Elizabeth I
Born: 1533
Crowned: 1558
Died: 1603
One of England's most famous monarchs. She was queen for 45 years.

Jane Seymour

King Edward VI
Born: 1537
Crowned: 1547
Died: 1553
Became king at just nine years old. He ruled for only six years.

The wives at a glance

	Married	Marriage ended	Beheaded
Catherine of Aragon	1509	1533	
Anne Boleyn	1533		1536
Jane Seymour	1536	1537	
Anne of Cleves	1540	1540	
Catherine Howard	1540		1542
Catherine Parr	1543	1547	

To remember what happened to each wife, you can use this rhyme:

*"**Divorced**, **beheaded**, died;*

Divorced, beheaded, survived."

However, the rhyme is not quite true, as Henry never got divorced. Instead, his marriages to Catherine of Aragon and Anne of Cleves were **annulled** (cancelled).

Glossary

annul cancel a marriage as if it never happened. Henry VIII had two of his marriages annulled.

behead chop off someone's head. In Tudor times, beheading was considered a good way to be executed.

chancellor senior assistant to a king or leader. The chancellor often deals with a country's money.

dissolution getting rid of or closing down. The dissolution of the monasteries meant shutting them down.

divorce end a marriage. In Henry's day, the Church did not allow divorce.

execute kill someone as a punishment. Long ago, people were often executed, even for small crimes.

executioner someone whose job is to execute (kill) people. In Henry's time, executioners used axes to chop off people's heads.

lady-in-waiting maid to a queen or other rich lady. Ladies-in-waiting were usually from rich families themselves.

mare female horse. Calling a woman a mare is rude, because it means she looks like a horse.

monarch king or queen. Long ago, the monarch made the laws and could have people executed.

monastery large house where monks live and work. Henry closed down monasteries so that he could steal their riches.

Pope leader of the Catholic Church. The Pope lives in the Vatican in Rome, Italy.

reign length of time that a king or queen is in power

Renaissance period of great exploration, art, and science in Europe, from about 1400 to 1650. Henry helped the Renaissance by paying money to artists and musicians.

sharp-tongued making quick, harsh comments

tax money that a country collects from its people. People often dislike paying taxes.

torture making someone suffer a lot of pain

treason plotting against your king or country. For many years, treason could be punished by death.

valuable worth a lot of money. Land is very valuable.

Want to know more?

Books to read

Brilliant Brits: Henry VIII, Richard Brassey (Orion, 2003)

Henry VIII (Discover the Tudors), Moira Butterfield (Franklin Watts, 2013)

Henry VIII and his Wicked Wives, Alan MacDonald (Scholastic, 2009)

Websites

www.tudorplace.com.ar/Documents/king_henryVIII_gallery.htm
Paintings and woodcuts showing Henry, his wives, his friends, and interesting scenes from his life.

www.bbc.co.uk/schools/primaryhistory/famouspeople/henry_viii/
Find out what it was like to be King in Tudor Britain!

www.show.me.uk/topicpage/Tudors.html
This website has links to interesting websites about the Tudors from museums all over the country.

www.hrp.org.uk/PalaceKids/discover/allabouttudors
Find out all about the Tudors at this website.

Index